# ANGEL IN I

# JO WALKER

ILLUSTRATED BY

# SARA JO FLOYD

PAGE PUBLISHING
Conneaut Lake, PA

First originally published by Page Publishing 2023

ISBN 978-1-6624-7357-9 (PBK)
ISBN 979-8-89157-530-1 (HBK)
ISBN 978-1-6624-7359-3 (DIGITAL)

Printed in the United States of America

# ANGEL IN DISGUISE

## JO WALKER

ILLUSTRATED BY

## SARA JO FLOYD

Hello sweet friend, I'm so glad you are here;
Don't move a muscle, don't you dare disappear.

I have a secret, yes you might be surprised;
But here is my announcement, "I'm an angel in disguise."

I know you might be wondering how this in fact is true,
But let me assure you, I'm not from out of the blue.

There is a master artist who doesn't make mistakes;
In fact, His awesome wonders include the mountains, the stars and the lakes.

So while I might look strange to you, with my one long and one tiny arm;
God alone, made me His child, filled with love and endless charm.

The greatest news that you should know is that I'm not the only one;
there are more like me; a sight to see; He designed us, everyone.

He made us each uniquely distinct to show His love for us;
Just look at some of my special friends, Lainey, Ruthie, Brady and Rus!

So don't be afraid when you see our faces in the store or at the park;
I hope you'll come over and say HELLO, and give a kind remark.

The only difference that you might see is our determination to finish the task, we may need some help from a loving friend, so we encourage you to ask.

We love to laugh and tell silly jokes and see your happy face;
we love to run and jump and skip and pretend we live in space.

Just like you, we love to play on the swings and slides outside, and just like you, we love to play hide and seek inside.

We also love to sing and dance and sometimes raise our voice;
we'll clap and stomp and lift our hands to praise with loud rejoice.

We are so much more than what you see, so often the world disagrees.
Our hearts are filled with eternal love, come meet us and you'll agree.

We all have our days of feeling alone, and I'm sure you have felt this too;
days when you cry and you're not sure why, days when you're feeling real blue.

Don't believe the lies that you're not enough in a world that sets the bar,
you are strong and brave and more than enough, you are the Lord's bright blazing star.

So take my advice, when the world feels cruel and continues to tell you lies;
Do as I do and yell out loud: "I'M AN ANGEL IN DISGUISE!"

# *About*
# SHANI

THIS BOOK IS DEDICATED TO OUR PRECIOUS DAUGHTER **SELAH "SHANI" WALKER**. In 2017, the Lord called us to consider adoption and in 2021, we were matched with our beautiful Indian princess. Although Shani was born with limb difference in both arms and scoliosis of the spine, she lets nothing hold her back. She is so incredibly smart, funny, motivated and extremely determined to succeed at anything she puts her mind to. Her life has been such a blessing to us and we are so thankful for the opportunity to love her forever.

**JO WALKER** WAS BORN IN BLOEMFONTEIN, SOUTH AFRICA. She has a bachelor's degree from Old Dominion University, a diploma in women's leadership from Columbia International University and is also a Licensed Massage Therapist. She is a proud wife and mother to three beautiful children. Her hobbies include running, pickleball, singing and spending quality time with family. Her desire is to inspire others to know their worth in Jesus and to find their purpose in life through Him.

Follow Shani's Journey on Instagram @WALKER_ADOPTION

## About the
# ILLUSTRATOR

**SARA JO FLOYD** STARTED ILLUSTRATING BOOKS AS A young girl. She would write short stories about her pets or the squirrels living in the attic and bring them to life with crayons. As Sara Jo grew, so did her love for painting, drawing, sewing, and creating with her hands. Being homeschooled on a Midwest farm meant she had lots of experience with her favorite furry subjects and more time to pursue her passion for art. It wasn't until she went to college that she got her first real art class. She went on to graduate with an art degree, and then taught art to school children, until she had her own. Sara Jo and her husband have two biological daughters and two daughters who were grafted into their family through adoption, both of which are blind. Now they homeschool their little women on their own Midwestern farm with 72 animals. They affectionately named this historic 1893 farmstead "Bryarton Farm." The bucolic views and peaceful setting are the perfect backdrop for Sara Jo to illustrate children's books as well as to teach her children.

Printed in the USA
CPSIA information can be obtained
at www.ICGtesting.com
CBHW041532250124
3748CB00024B/1190